From Shannon,
Christmas 2000
~ Canberra ~

Beverley Sutherland Smith's

Decadent Desserts

Beverley Sutherland Smith's

Decadent Desserts

SPRING, SUMMER, AUTUMN & WINTER

The Five Mile Press

Contents

Photographs on previous pages: Chocolate Mascarpone Indulgence (left), Almond and Chocolate Meringue (detail, right).

Introduction

I grew up in a household where desserts were abundant; they graced the table at almost every meal. Although they were not necessarily grand affairs, they were lovingly made from the best ingredients available at the time — limited though they may have been. There were trifles from yesterday's homemade swiss roll, laced with the brown sherry kept in the sideboard, and uneven bits of brightly-coloured chopped jelly. Then there were the baked bread and butter custards, with little sooty-coloured bits of chewy raisins dotting the top. When there were apples lying under the trees we ate aromatic, buttery apple pies, fluffy apple sponges and sugary apple slices. And, at the end of summer when passionfruit littered the ground, a passionfruit flummery served in an etched crystal bowl was a Sunday lunch treat; and the much-loved warm pudding, Lemon Delicious, became a speckled Passionfruit Delicious. Chocolate was reserved for special occasions, as were fruit or plum puddings. For easy desserts, and family occasions, ripe summer bananas were sliced into a puddle of runny cream and scattered with sticky brown sugar, or mixed with strawberries and fresh orange juice. The rhythm of the changing seasons of my childhood desserts still remains bright in my memory.

So many of the fruits that are now commonplace were never seen in those days, although we may perhaps have read about them or heard of them growing in grand gardens. Luscious tropical fruits, blueberries, stoned fruits of the highest quality — the range of produce now available is abundant and glorious. However, it is still sensible to make desserts from whatever you find at its best in the market at any particular time of year. This book follows a seasonal theme, beginning with spring when the weather is erratic and changes like passing moods. Cherries are the first symbol of spring, and several cherry dishes have been included. Berries are at their sharpest at that time of year, so need to be used with sweet combinations. Then in summer they should be left alone, so the glory of their perfume and flavour is not dulled. Summer desserts are light and fresh, the kind that can be eaten on a warm summer's day or sultry evening, while those of autumn bring warmth to the table. As for winter desserts, they should be downright hearty and comforting.

I have plucked out nostalgic dishes from the past, such as the queen of summer desserts, Summer Pudding, and the caramel-flavoured Orange and Date Sticky Pudding, which is perfect for winter's evenings. And I've given a new twist to some old classics, adding the nuts and fruits of autumn to a Harvest Pie, or simmering some sprigs of autumn basil in with pears poached in red wine. I have also included some classic desserts I have enjoyed on visits to other countries — for instance, Boston Cream Pie and the rum-soaked New Orleans Apple and Bourbon Pudding.

Most of us respond to the bright colours and sparkling flavours of desserts with a delight that, try as we may, is more difficult to provoke with a bowl of vegetables or a platter of meat. Most things in life have a beginning, middle and an end, and a well-chosen dessert is the perfect finish to a meal; and it is the course most likely to linger in the memory.

Beverley Sutherland Smith
Melbourne, 1996

Spring

A soft, pale season with pink buds on the blossom trees, deeper pink-to-red
plump cherries and tiny, lightly-coloured early strawberries,
spring brings gentle promise of the many treats in store
as the warmer weather unfolds.

Berry Meringue Cream

The sharp, slightly acid flavour of early berries makes an ideal combination with sweet meringue. A simple dessert, and one that comes in shades of pink, it should be served in your prettiest wine glasses and decorated with the most perfect of the berries from the punnet.
This makes 6 servings.

Berry cream
2 punnets (500 g) strawberries
1 cup cream
1 tablespoon sugar
1 tablespoon kirsch
6 large meringues

Meringues
3 egg whites
pinch salt
6 heaped tablespoons sugar
½ teaspoon vanilla essence
½ teaspoon vinegar

To make the berry cream
Reserve six strawberries, one for the top of each serve, and hull the rest. Cut one punnet of berries into slices.
Using a fork, roughly mash these on a plate.
Whip the cream until it holds stiff peaks and add the sugar. Mix in the mashed berries and kirsch.

To make the meringues
Put a sheet of non-stick baking paper on a flat tray.
Preheat the oven to slow (130°C).
Beat the egg whites with salt until they are stiff. Slowly add the sugar and continue beating until shiny. Add the vanilla and vinegar.
Using a dessertspoon, put spoonfuls of the mixture onto the tray, and bake for about 2 hours or until firm to the touch. They should be a pale creamy colour. Turn the oven off and let them cool in the oven. They can be stored in an airtight tin, and should keep well for about six weeks.

To assemble
Cut the remaining berries into halves or thick slices, depending on their size, and roughly crush up the meringues so they are in chunky pieces.
Put a few berries into the wine glasses, a spoonful of the strawberry cream, some chunks of meringue, more berries, cream and meringue, finishing with cream.
Put the reserved berry on the top and serve within about 20 minutes, while the meringue is still crunchy.

Cherry Clafoutis

During the cherry season in the French province of Limousin, a clafoutis or cherry flan is one of the traditional dishes for family meals. The classic versions have quite a high proportion of flour to eggs, and are rather like making a pancake batter and pouring it over fruit. This is a lighter variation, a buttery soft flan with a custard texture, scented with cognac or kirsch. It is still one of the nicest ways to enjoy cherries as a hot dessert, but like many egg dishes it should be rested for a while, once cooked, so it comes warm to the table rather than piping hot from the oven. This allows the full flavours to be truly appreciated. The cherry juices remain treacherously hot around the stone, even when the custard surrounding them has become tepid. So if you are impatient, and eat this dish too soon, be cautious.

You can also make the clafoutis with other fruits in season. Try pears, ripe plums, apricots, nectarines or peaches. The fruit should first be cut into slices and placed into the dish, to form a layer underneath the custard.

This makes a generous amount for 8–10 people. The recipe can be halved if you wish but don't bother halving a whole egg — just use two whole eggs and one egg yolk.

500 g dark red cherries
¼ cup sugar
2 tablespoons plain flour
pinch salt
3 eggs
2 egg yolks
2 cups milk
½ cup cream
3 tablespoons cognac, (or brandy or kirsch)
icing sugar

Method
Preheat the oven to moderate (180°C).
Generously butter a baking dish, such as a 20 cm pie or quiche dish. It should have a capacity of about five to six cups.
Remove the stalks from the cherries and spread them over the base. Mix the sugar with the flour and salt in a mixing bowl. Add the whole eggs and yolks and beat with a fork for a few seconds.
Mix in the milk, cream and cognac and stir well. Pour through a sieve over the top of the cherries.
Bake in a oven for about 40–45 minutes or until it is puffed and golden-brown. It will deflate slightly once out of the oven. Leave to rest for about 15 minutes, then sift a layer of icing sugar over the top and serve with some cream alongside.

Almond and Chocolate Meringue

Formed in the shape of a cake, this has the same crusty exterior as a pavlova and a soft marshmallow heart with a mix of roasted almonds, chocolate and coconut through the centre.

It is quite sweet so is best decorated with plain whipped cream and some scrolls of chocolate. You could also garnish it with fresh strawberries.

For a softer meringue leave the cream on for 12 hours, but eat it within an hour if you prefer the meringue to be crisp.

Enough for 8–10 serves.

90 g blanched almonds
60 g dark chocolate, finely chopped
$^1/_3$ cup desiccated coconut
3 large egg whites
$^1/_4$ teaspoon cream of tartar
1 cup castor sugar
2 teaspoons cornflour
1 teaspoon lemon juice
1 cup cream
75 g chocolate, cut into small pieces
2–3 strawberries (optional)

Method
Preheat the oven to moderate (180°C).
Butter a 20 cm cake tin. Line both the sides and base with non-stick baking paper and lightly butter it.
Put the almonds onto a baking tray or small container and roast in the oven until golden. Chop finely. (Don't put into a food-processor or they will become powdery and lose all their texture.) Mix with the chocolate and coconut.
Beat the egg whites with the cream of tartar until stiff. Very gradually add the castor sugar, beating until a thick meringue. Sift the cornflour over the top and add the lemon juice and mix through. Stir in the nuts and chocolate and spoon into the container.
Level the top and put into the oven for 30 minutes. Remove and carefully invert onto a flat tray which has a sheet of baking paper on it. The meringue should come out easily. Return to the oven. Turn it down to moderately slow (160°C) and continue cooking for a further 10 minutes or until very firm to the touch on the outside edges. Remove and leave to cool completely. You can keep it at this stage for 24 hours.
Whip the cream and pipe or spoon over the top of the meringue. Draw the blade of a knife through the cream to make ridges. Melt the chocolate in a basin over a pan of simmering water. Using a pastry bag with a ribbon tube, or a bag made from paper with a fine cut on the base, pipe back and forth to give a striped effect. Garnish with strawberries if you wish.

Rolled Black Forest Torte

In Jane Grigson's Fruit Book *the author aptly describes this cake as 'an extravaganza of chocolate whirls and curls, cream and cherries'. Originating in Germany, it is still featured all over the world. This particular version is quite different in that the cake is rolled into spirals so when wedges are cut the cake looks like the layered bark of a tree. But if you don't want to go to this bother, make three cakes in 22 cm sponge tins and layer these cakes with the cream and cherry mixture.*

The original version is quite heavy and very, very rich. This variation is based on a light chocolate sponge and the filling can be made with fresh poached cherries if they are in season. But it is just as good made with dark canned cherries that have been well drained. It must be made in advance and needs to rest for at least 12 hours before it is cut.

It makes 16 generous portions.

Chocolate cake
4 tablespoons plain flour
4 tablespoons cocoa
pinch salt
8 eggs
1 cup castor sugar
$^{1}/_{2}$ teaspoon cream of tartar

Syrup
$^{3}/_{4}$ cup water
$^{1}/_{3}$ cup sugar
2 tablespoons brandy
2 tablespoons kirsch

Filling
2 cups cream
1 teaspoons vanilla essence
750 g cooked cherries
  or 2 x 450 g cans pitted
  dark cherries, well drained

To finish the cake
additional 1 cup cream
1 tablespoon sugar
lots of chocolate shavings
  or curls
icing sugar (optional)

To make the cake
Butter the base of two swiss roll tins, 30 cm x 20 cm. Line the base and sides with non-stick baking paper. Lightly brush this again with some melted unsalted butter. (If you don't have two tins you can cook the mixtures, one after another. However the second one will not rise quite as high.)

Sift the flour with the cocoa and salt onto a piece of greaseproof paper. Separate the eggs and beat the whites with cream of tartar until stiff. Add the sugar and beat until glossy.

Mix the yolks with a whisk to break them up.

Add half of the flour and cocoa mixture. Then fold in a cup of egg whites, the remaining flour and cocoa and the rest of the egg whites.

Pour half the mixture into each swiss roll tin and level the top. Bake in a moderate oven, (180°C), for 18–20 minutes, or until firm to the touch.

Remove from the tin by lifting or sliding out the cake, still on the paper, and leave to cool. Do not remove the cakes from the paper as it makes them easier to handle when they are assembled.

To make the syrup

Heat the water and sugar until the sugar has dissolved, then turn up the heat and cook until reduced to half. Add the brandy and kirsch and allow to cool.

To make the filling and assemble

Whip the cream until it is stiff. Add the vanilla and mix through.

Cut one of the cakes into three long strips and then, using scissors, cut through the paper. It will still be attached. Brush one strip of cake with a little syrup, then spread with some cream and press some cherries into the cream.

Have the base of a spring-form tin or a pizza base ready, so that once the cake is assembled it can easily be inverted. Roll the cake strip up like a swiss roll, quite firmly peeling it away from the paper. Place in the centre of the tin. Take a second strip of cake and spread with syrup and cream, putting on some cherries. Lift this strip of cake on the paper and put around the outside of the first one, again carefully peeling away the paper. It will be a little messy but once chilled it will hold and you can easily tidy it. Continue until you have used up all the cake, cream and cherries, cutting the second cake into strips and continuing. Spread any cream that has oozed out on top of the cake. Cover lightly with some plastic-wrap and chill. Carefully invert the cake onto a plate and remove the metal base.

To finish

Whip the cream until it holds stiff peaks and add the sugar. Beat through. Spread over the top and sides of the cake. Cover generously with chocolate shavings or curls, or both.

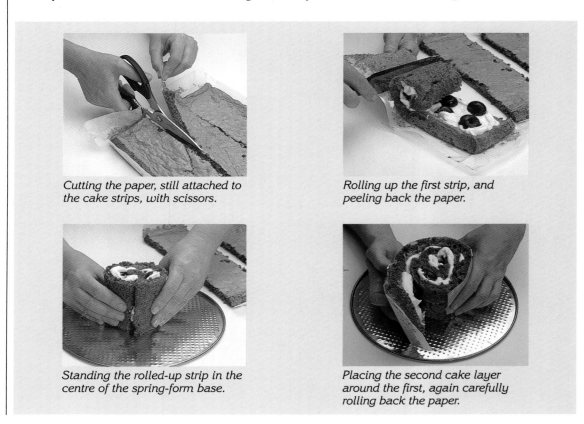

Cutting the paper, still attached to the cake strips, with scissors.

Rolling up the first strip, and peeling back the paper.

Standing the rolled-up strip in the centre of the spring-form base.

Placing the second cake layer around the first, again carefully rolling back the paper.

Chocolate Paradise

A rich, melt-in-the-mouth chocolate loaf, rather like a firm truffle in texture, Chocolate Paradise is decadently delicious. You could simply serve it with some whipped cream or you could spoon a sauce of puréed berries along with some fresh berries around it.
It keeps particularly well for up to five days, and serves 12 generously.

125 g dark chocolate, cut into small pieces
125 g milk chocolate, cut into small pieces
3 tablespoons brandy
250 g unsalted butter
¼ cup icing sugar

2 egg yolks
90 g ground almonds
2 egg whites

Method

Lightly butter the base and sides of a log container which holds about four cups. Line the base with a strip of non-stick baking paper, so it will be easier to turn out the chocolate loaf. Put both kinds of chocolate into a basin and leave to melt over a pan of simmering water. Stir until smooth.
Add the brandy and half of the butter, cut into small pieces. Mix well.
Cream the remaining butter with sugar until creamy. Add the egg yolks, one at a time, and then the chocolate, a little at a time, mixing in the ground almonds last.
Beat the egg whites until stiff, then gently fold them into the chocolate, a third at a time. Put into the container and smooth the top. Cover with a piece of plastic wrap. Chill for at least 6 hours. Unmould and cut into slices for serving, using a knife that has been run under hot water to give a clean edge.

Lime and Lemon Creams

Tart, fresh, with a pleasurably acid flavour and yet creamy at the same time, these little custards should be so softly set that they melt on your tongue. Limes are available from spring through to summer, but for times of year when they are not in season you can make this dish using two additional medium-sized lemons instead of the limes.

When grating the rind make sure you remove only the coloured section, which gives the desired citrus flavour. The pith is bitter. Candied peel is an optional but lovely accompaniment to the creams. This makes 8 individual serves.

Citrus creams
3 limes
1 lemon
2 cups milk
1 cup cream
4 eggs
3 egg yolks
1/3 cup castor sugar

Candied lime and lemon peel
2 limes
2 lemons
1 1/2 cups water
1 cup sugar
1 tablespoon brandy

To make the creams
Preheat the oven to moderate (180°C).
Lightly butter the base of the dishes and line each one with a circle of non-stick baking paper. Grate the rind of three limes and one lemon into a bowl.
Heat the milk and cream in a saucepan until it bubbles on the edges. Then add the lime and lemon peel and leave to rest for about 15 minutes.
Beat the eggs and yolks with sugar until thick, and pour the milk through a sieve over the top. Stir well.
Pour into the dishes and place them into a shallow container. Pour in hot water so that it comes about halfway up the custard dishes. Loosely cover the tops with foil and cook for about 20 minutes or until they are just set. Remove and leave to cool, then gently invert onto plates. Serve with candied lime and peel and some thick cream.

To candy the lime and lemon peel
Cut the limes and lemons (with the peel still on) into very thin slices.
Put into a pot of water and cook very gently for about 10 minutes. Drain and cover generously with fresh cold water and cook until completely tender. Drain carefully so as not to break the pieces too much.
Heat the water and sugar until the sugar has dissolved. Add the lime and lemon slices and leave over a low heat for about an hour, or until the peel on the slices is translucent and surrounded by a light syrup.
Pour into a bowl and add the brandy. Leave to rest for at least 4 hours. Remove the citrus slices from the syrup and arrange as a garnish.
It is inevitable that some of this will break up as it cooks, but this does not matter.
Any leftover can be stored for up to a month if left in the syrup in a glass jar.

Jubilant Cherries

A dish of drama and contrasts, piping hot cherries are poured around icy cold vanilla ice cream. Or for a more intensely cherry flavour, you could serve cherry ice cream, which keeps for about five days. This dessert is usually flamed but if you don't want the bother of this, just add the alcohol to the hot cherries and leave to cook for a minute. In many versions of this dish the cherries are stoned first but I rather like to leave the stones in so the fruit keeps a better shape. It will also have more flavour. These cherries reheat well so can be cooked a day in advance.

When served with ice cream, this makes enough for 6–8 people. But if you want to eat the hot cherries on their own it is only enough for 4.

Cherries
500 g large cherries
½ teaspoon grated orange rind
½ cup orange juice
1 cup red wine
1 cup water
½ cup sugar
piece of cinnamon stick about 2 cm long
1 tablespoon red currant jelly
1 tablespoon cornflour

Accompaniments
2 tablespoons kirsch or brandy
vanilla (or cherry) ice cream
a little whipped cream
scrolls of dark chocolate

To cook the cherries
Pull the stalks from the cherries.
Put the orange rind and juice into a saucepan with the red wine, water, sugar and cinnamon, and bring slowly to a boil. Cook gently, covered, for 10 minutes to allow the syrup to mellow. Add the cherries and leave covered over a very low heat for about 10 minutes or until they have softened. Add the red currant jelly and let it melt. Mix the cornflour with enough water to make a thin paste. Add a couple of spoonfuls of the hot cherry juice and then stir this back into the cherries. Keep stirring until the sauce thickens slightly. Allow to cool and refrigerate, covered, if not using immediately. If you intend to serve the cherries instantly, allow to cool for a minute.

To serve
Put a scoop of ice cream into shallow bowls. Heat the kirsch or brandy and add to the cherries. Then immediately put into plates, adding plenty of sauce around the ice cream, making sure each person receives a good equal proportion of cherries.
Put a tiny spoonful of cream on the top of the ice cream and decorate with some dark chocolate scrolls or grated chocolate.

Cherry Ice Cream

500 g ripe dark cherries
$\frac{1}{4}$ cup water
1 tablespoon sugar
2 strips orange rind
1 teaspoon red currant jelly

$1\frac{1}{4}$ cups cream
3 egg yolks
$\frac{2}{3}$ cup sugar
$\frac{1}{2}$ teaspoon vanilla essence

Method

Stone the cherries. There is no way around this as the ice cream needs to have a coarsely chopped mixture of cherries as its base. Put the cherries into a saucepan with the water, sugar and orange rind. Cook very gently until they are soft, and then add the red currant jelly and stir until dissolved. Leave to cool for 5 minutes, then put the entire mixture into a food-processor and blend to a pulp. Let cool completely.

Heat the cream until little bubbles form on the edges.

Beat the yolks with sugar until thick and pale and gradually tip in the hot cream, stirring all the time. Return the mixture to the saucepan and cook until it is very slightly thickened, being careful not to allow it to boil. Remove from the heat and add the vanilla. Let cool and mix with the cherry pulp.

Freeze in an ice cream machine or in a tray in the freezer, stirring several times to make sure the fruit doesn't sink to the base. Cover well.

Lemon Brûlée Tart

With its buttery crust and sharp, tangy but creamy filling, this lemon tart is irresistible.
If you want to give your tart a brûlée topping you'll need a really hot griller.
This tart will keep for a couple of days but is best of all consumed within 24 hours.
This cuts into 10 portions.

Pastry
1¼ cups plain flour
pinch salt
2 tablespoons castor sugar
125 g butter, cut into small
  pieces
1 egg yolk
2 tablespoons lemon juice
  or water

Lemon filling
4 eggs
1 cup castor sugar
grated rind 2 large lemons
⅓ cup orange juice
⅓ cup lemon juice
⅓ cup cream

Brûlée topping
2 tablespoons icing sugar

To make the pastry
Preheat the oven to 180°C.
Lightly butter the base of a 23 cm tart tin with a removable base.
Put the flour, salt, sugar and butter into a food-processor and blend until crumbly. Add
the egg yolk and lemon juice and process to a ball.
Flatten out, wrap in some plastic-wrap and leave to rest for 20 minutes. Roll out between
some waxed paper and press onto the base and sides of a 23 cm tart base. You may have
a little over. If so, discard it. It is important that the crust not be too thick on the base, but
thick enough on the sides to hold the lemon filling. Lightly butter a sheet of foil and
press, buttered side down, onto the base and sides of the case and bake in the preheated
oven for about 20 minutes or until set. Very carefully remove the foil and return to the
oven for a further 5–10 minutes so the base dries out. Cool while making up the filling.

To make the filling
Beat the eggs and sugar until light. Then add the lemon rind and both orange and lemon
juice and mix. Stir in the cream last. Pour the mixture into the case, but not right to the
top. Place the tart in the oven and now, using a small jug, pour the remaining filling in.
This way it is less likely to spill over the edges. Bake in the oven for about 20 minutes or
until barely set. It will firm more as it cools. Leave to cool.

To make the brûlée topping
Cut a sheet of foil to make a circle a little larger than the pie. Now cut out (and discard) a
smaller circle, leaving you with a foil ring to protect the crust.
Preheat the griller. Rest the foil carefully on top of the pastry, dull side upwards,
and — using a sieve — scatter the centre of the tart with a fine layer of sugar.
Grill until golden and remove immediately. Allow to cool, then remove the sides from the
tin and slide from the base.

Lime Delicious

Whoever named this dessert chose aptly; it is indeed delicious. This much-loved dish, which dates back to the middle of this century, was more often made with lemons, and was called Lemon Delicious. This is a more sophisticated version of the old family favourite, the addition of limes giving an added sharpness and tang.

Early limes are bright green, and don't have as much juice as they do when they lose some of their vibrant colour and turn a greenish-gold. If you wish to keep the distinctive flavour of the lime on hand for special dishes — beyond the lime season — you can squeeze some juice into small ice-block containers and freeze it for several months. The same can be done if you have a surplus of lemons.

This light and easy dessert serves 6.

60 g butter
¾ cup castor sugar
grated rind of 2 limes
grated rind of 1 small lemon
3 eggs
3 tablespoons plain flour
½ cup milk
2–3 tablespoons lime juice, depending on personal taste
¼ cup lemon juice
icing sugar for dusting the top

Method
Butter the base of an ovenproof dish that holds four cups.
Preheat the oven to moderately slow (160°C).
Cream the butter with the sugar, lime and lemon rind until very light and fluffy. Separate the eggs and add the yolks, one at a time, to the creamed base. Sift the flour over the top and stir through.
Mix the milk with the lime and lemon juices and stir into the mixture.
Beat the egg whites until they hold very stiff peaks.
Fold in, a third at a time, through the lime base.
Pour the mixture into the buttered dish and smooth the top.
Place the pudding into a baking tin and pour enough boiling water around it, so that it comes halfway up the dish. Bake in the oven for about 45 minutes or until it is just firm to touch on top. Before serving, dust with icing sugar. This pudding should be served hot or warm. It reheats quite well in a microwave.

Boston Cream Pie

Not a pie at all, this is a famous American dessert cake. It consists of two layers of fluffy light sponge filled with a rich brandy custard, with a truffle-textured chocolate icing trickling over the edges.

Much of the preparation can be done in advance. You can make the cake layers the day before, and the custard keeps well for three days. And once assembled, the Boston Cream Pie can be refrigerated for 24 hours.

Leave it out about an hour before serving so it is not too cold.

This cake cuts into 8–10 generous wedges.

Cake
6 eggs
²/₃ cup sugar
¹/₂ cup cornflour
¹/₄ cup plain flour
1¹/₂ teaspoons baking
 powder
pinch salt
1 tablespoon melted butter
1 teaspoon vanilla essence

Custard filling
1¹/₂ cups cream
³/₄ cup milk
5 egg yolks
¹/₂ cup castor sugar
3 tablespoons cornflour
1 teaspoon vanilla essence
3 tablespoons brandy

Chocolate truffle topping
¹/₃ cup cream
30 g unsalted butter
125 g dark chocolate, cut
 into tiny pieces

To make the cake
Preheat the oven to moderate (180°C).
Brush the base and sides of two sponge sandwich tins or cake tins, 23 cm in diameter, with a little melted butter. Line the base, of both with non-stick baking paper.
Separate the eggs and beat the whites until stiff. Add the sugar and beat for about 3 minutes with an electric beater until very glossy and stiff.
Mix in the yolks, one at a time, and sift the cornflour, plain flour, baking powder and salt over the top. Fold through, lastly folding in the butter and vanilla.
Divide equally between the two tins and bake for about 20 minutes or until firm to the touch on top. The cakes will shrink slightly away from the sides of the tins.
Leave to cool for 5 minutes and then gently run a knife around the edge and invert onto a cake-rack to cool.

To make the custard
Heat the cream with milk until bubbles form around the edge. Beat the yolks with sugar, using a whisk, and add the cornflour. Slowly pour the hot creamy milk over the top, stirring as you do so. Return to the saucepan. Cook the mixture, stirring continually until it has thickened. Remove from the heat and add the vanilla and brandy. Leave to cool, but you will need to give it a stir every so often to prevent a skin forming on top of the custard. Covered, in the refrigerator, this keeps for up to three days.

Note: For a firmer custard filling, add one teaspoon of gelatine dissolved in water while custard is still warm.

Summer

*Berries are the essence of this season: aromatic strawberries,
frosted blueberries, purple blackberries and the fragile queen of them all,
raspberries. But other joys of summer are stoned and tropical fruits.
Summer is a true celebration of
the bounty of nature.*

Apricot Almond Pudding

Apricots, with their tart, tangy flavour, rest under a puffy coat of ground almond pudding. Serve this dessert plain, or with a sauce made from the apricot syrup, and accompanied by a generous bowl of whipped cream.
It makes ample for 8.

Pudding
750 g apricots
$^1/_2$ cup water
$^2/_3$ cup sugar
piece of vanilla bean
  or 1 teaspoon vanilla essence
90 g ground almonds
$^1/_4$ cup castor sugar
4 egg yolks
$^1/_2$ teaspoon vanilla essence
1 tablespoon apricot or plain brandy
4 egg whites
4 tablespoons castor sugar
$^1/_4$ cup flaked almonds

Sauce
$^1/_3$ cup smooth apricot jam
$^2/_3$ cup syrup from cooking the apricots
$^1/_3$ cup sugar
2 tablespoons brandy
2 teaspoons cornflour

To make the pudding
Cut the apricots into halves and remove the stones. Put the apricots into a saucepan with the water, sugar and vanilla bean or essence. Cook gently until they are tender, but be careful they don't break. Remove them with a slotted spoon to a shallow ovenproof dish which holds about four-and-a-half cups
Heat the oven to moderate (180°C).
Put the almonds, sugar, yolks, vanilla and brandy into a bowl. Stir well.
Beat the whites until they hold stiff peaks. Gradually add the sugar and beat until very stiff. Fold about a third at a time into the yolks.
Spoon over the apricots and lightly cover with almonds. Bake in the preheated oven for about 25 minutes or until puffy and golden on top.

To make the sauce
Mix the jam with the liquid from the apricots and the sugar. Cook for about 3 minutes, stirring occasionally. Remove and add the brandy. Mix the cornflour with enough water to make a thin paste and add to the mixture. Return to the heat and stir until it has lightly thickened. Serve with the pudding.

Plum Dessert Cake

Richly textured, with lashings of butter to lend a soft, melting taste, this cake is topped with bright, juicy plum quarters which leave lovely syrupy sections through the topping. The best plums of all to use in this dessert are the vividly-coloured blood plums. As a change, when plenty of stoned fruits are in season, you could try ripe nectarines or peaches instead.

Cream, and lots of it, is the best accompaniment for those who don't suffer from guilt. But if you do, this cake with its great rustic country flavours is marvellous on its own.

It cuts into 8 or more portions and keeps for days.

125 g butter
½ cup sugar
pinch nutmeg
pinch cinnamon
½ teaspoon lemon rind
2 eggs
1 tablespoon sour cream or milk
½ cup self-raising flour
2 tablespoons plain flour
500 g ripe but firm plums

Method
Preheat the oven to moderate (180°C).
Butter the sides and base of a 23 cm spring-form tin.
Cream the butter with the sugar, nutmeg, cinnamon and lemon rind until light and fluffy.
Beat the eggs and add a little at a time, then mix in the sour cream or milk. Sift both kinds of flour over the top of the batter.
Stir for 30 seconds with a wooden spoon. Spread over the cake tin base. The cake will rise as it cooks, but at this stage will be only a thin layer.
Cut the fruit into quarters and press, cut-side-down, into the cake base. Bake in the preheated oven for 45 minutes or until the cake is cooked and the fruit soft and syrupy.
It will look quite brown on the edges, but be sure to check it is cooked in the centre by inserting a fine skewer. If it is clean when removed, the cake is cooked.
Remove from the oven and let rest for 10 minutes before removing the sides of the tin. Serve warm or at room temperature.

Melted Blueberries and Nut Crunch

Blueberries are cooked so they soften and melt in the pan, forming just a little purple juice. Topped with cream and a wonderful nutty crunch, they form a contrast of hot and cold, and tart and sweet flavours.
Make the nut crunch first so it is well chilled.
This makes ample for 4 people.

Nut crunch
60 g unsalted butter
1 cup white or brown breadcrumbs, made
  from stale bread
1/3 cup sugar
1/4 cup chopped almonds or
  macadamia nuts
1/4 cup grated chocolate

Melted blueberries
1/4 cup water
1 tablespoon sugar
1 tablespoon Cointreau
1 tablespoon brandy
1 punnet blueberries

To finish the dessert
1/2 cup cream, whipped until very stiff

To make the nut crunch
Melt the butter in a large frying pan. Add the crumbs and toss with a fork until they begin to become slightly crisp and golden. Scatter on the sugar and cook until you have a deep golden mixture. Watch constantly, so it does not catch and burn on the base. Add the nuts and mix through, then remove from the heat and spread out onto a tray to cool. Mix in the chocolate, and separate with a fork if it has formed clumps.
Store in a screwtop jar in the refrigerator, where it can be kept for a week.

To cook the blueberries
Heat the water and sugar until the sugar has dissolved, then add the Cointreau, brandy and blueberries. Shake over the heat until they have begun to soften and melt in the syrup. It takes about 5 minutes. The skins should just slightly split. Remove immediately and chill.

To serve
Divide the blueberries and their juices between four individual dishes or glasses. Top with cream, then scatter a thick layer of the nut crunch on top. You will have more than you need, but the rest can be stored in the refrigerator.

Summer Pudding

Summer Pudding, with plenty of cream, is one of the most delectable summer desserts of all. It is never too sweet and never too heavy to finish off a dinner — as long as it includes a good proportion of raspberries and is made with proper bread. By 'proper' bread I mean a white country-style loaf. This will not become stodgy in the way that commercially-sliced bread does in this dish. It is always difficult to state exactly how much bread you will need, but buy a 500 g white loaf and you will probably find, after trimming off the crusts, you use about half to two-thirds of this.

Modelled on the Summer Pudding which Anton Mosimann created many years ago at the Dorchester, the berries are put into warm water and sugar until the juices run. This creates ample syrup to soak the bread layers. Just enough gelatine is used to give the pudding a good shape without making it too firm.

While raspberries are the one berry you must use, the other kinds can vary according to what is available. Blackberries, boysenberries, loganberries, blueberries, black currants, red currants — these are all wonderful. Many people prefer to leave out strawberries, but they are fine used in this particular version.

This makes 8 serves.

---

slices of white bread, crusts removed
1 teaspoon gelatine
½ cup water
½ cup sugar
500 g raspberries
250 g strawberries, hulled
250 g other berries, e.g. blackberries, mulberries, etc. but not blueberries

Method
Select a pudding basin which holds approximately six cups. Line the base with a piece of foil so the pudding can be easily removed.
Mix the gelatine with two tablespoons of the water. Stir well.
Put the remaining water and sugar into a saucepan and heat slowly until the sugar has dissolved. Now turn up the heat a little until the edges of the pan are bubbling, then remove instantly from the heat and add the gelatine, stirring to dissolve.
Cut the strawberries into halves and add to the syrup, along with the other berries and stir gently. Allow to cool.
Line the sides and base of the bowl with some pieces of bread so they fit quite snugly. They may overlap slightly. Spoon some berries and a little juice into the bread-lined container.
Cover over with a layer of bread and add more berries and a little more juice. Repeat once more, ending with a covering layer of bread. If the bread on the sides extends up beyond the final layer of bread, now is a good time to carefully trim the excess height away, as this bread will remain dry.

Triple Berry Tart

This tart is a celebration of summer and the berry season. A variety of berries of contrasting colours and flavours sit on a light almond crust. Unlike many such tarts, it has no cream base, so it is quite light and fresh if eaten plain. For the more indulgent, it can be served with cream. It cuts into 8–10 slices.

Biscuit base
185 g butter
1/3 cup sugar
60 g ground almonds
1 teaspoon vanilla essence
2 egg yolks
1 1/2 cups plain flour

Filling
3/4 cup red currant jelly
2 punnets (500 g) small strawberries
1 punnet (250 g) blueberries
1 punnet (250 g) raspberries
some icing sugar

To make the base
Put a sheet of non-stick baking paper onto a flat tray and mark out a circle with a diameter of about 22 cm.
Preheat the oven to moderate (180°C).
Cream the butter with the sugar, add the ground almonds and vanilla, and mix well. Now add the egg yolks and flour and mix to a dough. Knead for about 30 seconds and form into a ball. Wrap in some plastic-wrap and chill for 10 minutes. Reserve about a quarter of the pastry, then roll out the remainder between waxed paper to make a circle. Put onto the non-stick paper on the baking tray. If the dough is not a good shape, using your hands, gently push it to the edge of the marked-out circle. Prick the base lightly. Roll the reserved mixture out to form 'sausage' strips and put around the outside of the base to give a little edge. Pinch with your thumb and forefinger, pressing down firmly. Bake for about 15–20 minutes or until a deep golden colour, and quite crisp. Remove and leave to cool on the tray. Carefully transfer to a flat plate. You can use the baking paper as a support.

To make the filling and assemble the tart
Warm the red currant jelly, giving it a good stir every so often until it is smooth. Brush a layer over the base of the tart, and leave to set. Reserve the rest of the jelly for the top of the fruit. Hull the strawberries but don't wash any of the berries to avoid bruising them. Arrange the strawberries around the edge, then add the blueberries, piling the raspberries into the centre. Warm any leftover jelly and just lightly dab this on top of the berries.
Just before serving, dust the edges of the tart with sifted icing sugar.
Once filled, this tart is best eaten within 6 hours or the berries will begin to leak their juices into the pastry.
Hint: This is a very buttery, short base and will be quite sticky to roll, so it is essential to do this between waxed paper rather than on a floured bench. To make it easier to form the 'sausage' for the edge you can knead in an additional two tablespoons of flour which will give it more body. Handle the base carefully, once cooked, and be sure to decorate on the serving platter.

Tropical Cream

A mix of puréed tropical fruits form the base for a light, almost sticky baked cream mould. Served with more tropical fruits in an aromatic spiced ginger sauce, it sings of sunshine and balmy breezes.
This makes 8 small moulds. They keep well for several days.

500 g papaya
½ cup sugar
¼ cup lime juice
4 passionfruit
45 g unsalted butter, cut into small pieces
3 tablespoons cornflour
4 eggs
1 teaspoon vanilla essence

Method
Peel the papaya and take out the seeds. Roughly cut up the fruit and put into a saucepan with the sugar and lime juice. Bring to a boil and cook over very low heat for about 6 minutes with a lid partly covering the saucepan. The fruit should be very soft. Purée in a food-processor and add the passionfruit pulp to the warm papaya. Put the butter pieces into a bowl and push the pulp through a sieve over the top of the butter. Mix together — the butter should have melted.
Beat the cornflour and eggs until frothy and add the papaya and passionfruit pulp.
Lightly butter eight small soufflé or individual containers and line the base with non-stick baking paper. Spoon in the mixture. Bake in a moderate oven (180°C) for about 25 minutes or until it is set on the edges. The centre should be creamy. Leave to cool for at least an hour before inverting onto plates.

Tropical Fruit Salad

¼ cup water
juice of 1 lime
1 tablespoon ginger shreds
½ cinnamon stick
6 cardamon pods, lightly crushed
¼ teaspoon black pepper, coarsely ground

½ cup sugar
1 mango, cut into chunky pieces
2 passionfruit
4 or 5 slices pineapple, peeled and cut into
  wedges

Method
Put the water, lime, spices and sugar into a saucepan and bring to a boil. Leave to stand until cold and strain through a very fine sieve into a bowl. Add the mango, passionfruit pulp and pineapple and stir. Chill for several hours or for up to 12 hours.
Any fruits can be added to this — lychees, star fruit or whatever is in season.

Peach Tatin

The Tatin sisters covered caramelised apples with a crust, and turned it upside-down to make it one of the most famous French apple dishes. In this version the crust encloses sticky, glazed peaches to give a dish with rustic charm and sunny flavours. It begs for cream alongside and, if you really want to indulge, pure or clotted cream is best of all. This cuts into 8–10 portions.

Peaches	Caramel	Crust
1 kg firm yellow peaches	½ cup sugar	1½ cups plain flour
45 g butter	¼ cup water	3 tablespoons castor sugar
3 tablespoons white sugar		½ teaspoon baking powder
2 tablespoons brown sugar		pinch salt
		125 g butter
		1 egg yolk
		1 tablespoon water
		1 teaspoon vanilla

To cook the peaches
Peel the peaches and cut into quarters. Melt the butter in a frying pan, and add both kinds of sugar and the peaches. Toss over the heat, turning the peaches over until they have softened. However, don't let them collapse completely.

To make the caramel and assemble
Put the sugar and water into a metal saucepan and heat gently. Shake the pan occasionally until the sugar has dissolved and then turn up the heat and cook until it is a caramel colour. Butter a shallow cake tin, 23 cm in size, and as soon as the syrup has turned to caramel pour it into the tin.
Coat the base of the cake tin by tilting it to give an even layer.
Arrange the peaches, cut-side-down, in a layer over the caramel.

To make the pastry
Put the flour, with the sugar, baking powder, salt and butter, into a food-processor and blend until crumbly. It takes about 10 seconds. Then add the egg yolk, water and vanilla and process to a dough. Turn out and knead lightly. Form into a ball and leave to rest for 10 minutes, then roll out between waxed paper. Cut the pastry into a circle which is just a bit larger than the cake tin and press it over the top, pushing lightly on the edges and trimming the excess away.
Bake the tart in a moderate oven (180°C) for about 30 minutes, then turn the heat to low (150°C) and cook for a further 10 minutes.
Before inverting, leave to rest for 5 minutes.
Invert the tin onto the serving plate and give the base a tap to remove the fruit. Sometimes bits stick here and there, but it is quite easy to remove these with a knife and place them back on top. If there is any syrupy caramel in the tin pour this over. Serve hot or warm.

Raspberry Meringue Cake

The meringue topping forms little caps which hold the sifted icing sugar in a snowy coat over their golden-brown peaks. The cake underneath, made with egg yolks and cream, is richer than a sponge cake and lighter than a butter cake. Its textures and flavours provide a foil for the topping.

Sandwiched with cream and tart raspberries, some crushed to release deep rose juices here and there, it is a cake of great charm in both looks and taste.

It is exquisite if eaten on the day it is made, but keeps well for 24 hours. Be sure the meringue is thoroughly cooked, however, so it does not sweat.

Once creamed, of course, it must be refrigerated. But I find that it is best taken out of the refrigerator for about an hour before serving, so the cake is not too firm and cold.

This makes 6 serves.

Cake base
90 g butter
rounded $^1/_3$ cup castor sugar
5 egg yolks
1 teaspoon vanilla essence
$^1/_3$ cup plain flour
2 tablespoons cornflour
2 teaspoons baking powder
$^1/_4$ cup cream

Meringue topping
5 egg whites
1 cup castor sugar
1 teaspoon vanilla essence

Raspberry filling
2 punnets (500 g) raspberries
  (1 punnet will do)
1 cup cream
1 tablespoon icing sugar
$^1/_2$ teaspoon vanilla essence

To finish the cake
some cinnamon
icing sugar

To make the cake
Preheat the oven to barely moderate (170°C).

Butter the sides and base of two 23 cm cake tins. Line the base of each one with a piece of non-stick baking paper. Lightly butter this.

Cream the butter with the sugar until light and fluffy. Beat the yolks and add a little at a time, beating well. Add the vanilla and cream and mix through. Sift the flour, cornflour and baking powder over the top, and also mix through. Divide the mixture equally and spread into both tins. These layers will be very, very thin.

To make the meringue
Beat the egg whites until they are stiff, and gradually add the sugar, beating until a meringue. Add the vanilla last and mix through.

Spread this meringue evenly over the layers of cake and smooth the top. Bake in the preheated oven for about 35 minutes.

The meringue will be quite a deep colour and the cake must be cooked. Check by inserting a fine skewer if you are not sure. If it comes out clean, the cake is ready.

Leave the cakes in the tins for an hour and carefully invert onto a sheet of foil or non-stick baking paper rather than a rack, which could damage the meringue.

To make the filling
Put half the berries onto a plate and crush very lightly. Whip the cream until stiff, add the sugar and vanilla and mix in the crushed berries.

To assemble
Put one of the cakes onto a platter, meringue-side-down. Cover with the raspberry cream and arrange the remainder of the whole raspberries on top. Onto this, add the second layer of cake — this time, meringue-side-upwards.

Scatter the top with a little cinnamon and some sifted icing sugar. Leave for a couple of hours for the cake to mellow. Once assembled, it is best eaten within about 24 hours.

Spreading the cake mixture in a thin layer over the base.

Spreading the meringue mixture evenly over the cake mixture.

Loosening round the edges with a sharp knife.

The inverted cake, meringue-side-down.

Peaches in Rose Sauterne Sauce

With the curve of peaches shining through the surface of its glistening rose-coloured syrup, this is the most exquisite of summer desserts — the best one of all to choose after a rich main course, or in fact after any kind of course. Use a good Australian sauterne. This is enough for 6 serves.

1 cup water
¾ cup sugar
3 cups sauterne
4 strips lemon rind
6–9 medium-sized to small yellow peaches
1 punnet (250 g) raspberries

Method
Heat the water with the sugar in a large wide saucepan until the sugar has dissolved.
Add the sauterne and lemon rind and slide in the unpeeled peaches. Cover and leave to simmer over a very low heat until they can easily be pierced with a fork.
Carefully remove with a slotted spoon.
Add the raspberries to the hot sauce and leave to steep for about 15 minutes.
As soon as they are cool enough to handle, gently slip the skins from the peaches, using your fingers, and place in a bowl.
Pour the liquid from the saucepan over the top through a fine sieve, pressing down gently to get any additional juice from the raspberries. Chill for at least 6 hours.

Frozen Strawberry Mousse with Marshmallow

This tart, frozen strawberry mousse has cloud-like chunks of marshmallow studded with green pistachio nuts — a combination that will please all kids, the young ones and the young at heart.
It makes 10 servings and keeps well for several days.

Marshmallow	*Frozen strawberry mousse*	*Accompaniment* (optional)
$\frac{1}{2}$ cup sugar	2 punnets	1 punnet
$\frac{1}{2}$ cup water	(500 g) strawberries	(250 g) strawberries
2 teaspoons gelatine	$1\frac{1}{4}$ cups castor sugar	2 tablespoons castor sugar
1 tablespoon water	2 tablespoons lemon juice	1 tablespoon lemon juice
1 tablespoon lemon juice	$1\frac{1}{2}$ cups cream	
few drops vanilla essence		
$\frac{1}{3}$ cup pistachio nuts		

To make the marshmallow
Line the base of a shallow container, about 20 cm in size, with foil and lightly oil it.
Put the sugar and water into a saucepan, and stir over the heat until the sugar has dissolved. Mix the gelatine and water and stir, pour into the sugar syrup and bring to a boil. Cook gently for 10 minutes. It should form a ball when dropped into a cup of cold water. Add the vanilla and lemon juice and remove from the heat. Leave to become cold and then beat with an electric mixer until it is fluffy and white. Mix in the pistachio nuts. Pour the marshmallow into the foil-lined container and smooth the surface. Leave to set in the refrigerator. Chop into pieces of about 2.5 cm.

To make the strawberry mousse
Line the base of a large log tin, about 25 cm x 8 cm in size, with a strip of foil to make it easier to remove the mousse.
Hull three-quarters of the berries, keeping aside half a punnet for garnishing. Put into a food-processor with the sugar and lemon juice and blend to a purée. Whip the cream in a large bowl and gently fold in first the strawberry purée and then the marshmallow.
Pour or tip into the container, smooth the top and freeze until set. Cover with some plastic-wrap once it is frozen.

To serve
Either cut into slices or take out scoops with a large tablespoon. You can serve with a berry sauce made by blending a punnet of strawberries in a food-processor with two tablespoons castor sugar and a tablespoon lemon juice until a coarse purée.

Stuffed Nectarines with Almond Custard

Based on an Italian dish usually prepared with peaches, this is made with large sweet nectarines. It could however be made with pears or peaches.
The filling has an almond caramel flavour and the custard is made with fresh almonds to give the most aromatic and delicate of flavours.
It is important to use ripe but firm fruit or it will not cook through in the time it takes for the filling to bake. If your nectarines are not ripe you could cook them for a few minutes first before using in this dessert. This makes 8 servings.

Nectarines
¹/₃ cup blanched almonds
8 large ripe nectarines
a little lemon juice
125 g unsalted butter
2 tablespoons brown sugar
2 egg yolks
1 tablespoon Marsala
8 amaretti biscuits, crushed
2 tablespoons fine breadcrumbs
  made from stale white bread

Almond custard
1 cup unblanched almonds
¹/₂ cup milk
1 cup cream
¹/₃ cup sugar
4 egg yolks
2 teaspoons cornflour or arrowroot
1 tablespoon brandy

To prepare stuffed nectarines
Put the almonds into a moderate oven (180°C) on a flat tray and cook until they are a golden-brown colour. Remove and chop roughly.
Cut the nectarines into halves and remove the stones and then scoop out enough flesh to give a good-sized cavity. Squeeze a little lemon into the cavity so it does not discolour.
Chop the butter into small pieces and cream with the sugar until fluffy. Now add the yolks and mix well. Stir in the Marsala, amaretti biscuits, crumbs and toasted chopped nuts. Blend everything well. Brush a shallow ovenproof container with a little butter.
Stuff the centre of each nectarine with some of the filling. Put them into the dish and bake in the oven for about 20–25 minutes; timing will depend on the nectarines. The fruit should be soft, the filling golden-brown on top.

To make the almond custard
Put the almonds into the oven on a flat tray to toast. Chop finely. Heat the milk and cream and add the sugar and almonds. Remove from the heat and let stand for at least an hour. Strain the milk and cream into a bowl, pressing down well on the almonds to extract all the flavours. Having done this, discard the almonds.
Heat the milk and cream again. Beat the yolks with cornflour in a bowl and gradually add the hot milk and cream. Stir and return to the saucepan, stirring over a medium heat until it is lightly thickened. Don't allow it to boil. Remove and add the brandy. This custard can be kept for 48 hours. It can be carefully rewarmed in a basin standing over hot water, or in a microwave.

Autumn

Crisp, fresh textures are an indication that the balmy days of summer have gone, with crunchy apples, earthy, sweet-flavoured nuts and pears tinged red and gold — toning with the vibrant burst of autumn colours in the trees.

Glazed Grape Tart with Almond Crust

The perfect almond crust, combined with a sour cream and scented ginger filling and fresh, crisp grapes, makes this a very special tart.
It will cut into 10 slices.

Almond crust
1¼ cups plain flour
2 tablespoons icing sugar
155 g butter, diced small
45 g ground almonds
1 whole egg
1 tablespoon chilled water if necessary
 (or lemon juice)

Filling
½ cup apricot jam
¾ cup sour cream, mascarpone
 or thick pure cream
1 tablespoon fresh ginger juice (see Note)
1 tablespoon icing sugar
125 g large green seedless grapes
125 g dark grapes
an additional ½ cup apricot jam
1 tablespoon lemon juice
1 tablespoon brandy

To make the crust
Put the flour, icing sugar and butter into a food-processor and blend until mealy. Add the almonds and the egg and process again until it holds a shape. If it does not form a ball, quickly add chilled water or lemon juice. Remove and roll into a ball, then flatten down and wrap in some plastic. Leave to rest for 30 minutes. Roll out between waxed paper and put into a 25 cm flan tin. If the pastry is too soft to roll you can just press it in. Prick the base lightly. Butter some foil and press, buttered-side-down, into the case. It should extend up the sides. Bake in a moderate oven (180°C) for 20–25 minutes until firm. Carefully peel away the foil and continue baking for a further 10 minutes or until crisp and golden-brown. Leave to cool.

To make the filling
Warm the jam and push through a sieve. Brush the base with the jam and leave to set. Mix the sour cream with the ginger juice and icing sugar, stirring or whisking until well blended, and carefully spread over the jam. Cut the grapes into halves and if they have seeds flick them out. Arrange the grapes in alternating green and purple circles. Heat the additional jam with lemon juice, and cook for a couple of minutes. Add the brandy and cook again for a minute. Sieve into a bowl. Carefully brush over the top of the grapes and allow to cool or chill for about an hour.
This tart should be eaten on the day it is made, preferably within 8 hours of it being assembled. However, you can make up the crust in advance.

Note: To make the fragrant ginger juice grate about 4 cm of fresh ginger into a small bowl. Squeeze between your fingers into another small bowl and strain into the cream. If you have more than needed, store in a screwtop jar in the refrigerator and use in stir-fry dishes or as a digestif.

Raspberry and Fig Gratin

The second crop of raspberries coincides with the season for big, plump, purple figs. They make for a sensational duo when combined and coated with cream, sprinkled with brown sugar and quickly placed under a hot grill until the cream has melted and the sugar is caramelised. Heavenly flavours and very easy.
Serves 4.

8 ripe figs
1 punnet (250 g) raspberries
1 tablespoon brandy
1 tablespoon brown sugar
grated rind of 1 small orange
1 cup cream, whipped until stiff
additional soft brown sugar

Method
Carefully peel the figs and cut them into four pieces.
Scatter raspberries over the base of four small gratin dishes. Push the figs into the raspberries, so you have as even a layer as possible. Mix the brandy with brown sugar and scatter a little on top of the figs.
Stir the orange rind into the cream and spread evenly over the top. Refrigerate for up to 6 hours.
Preheat the griller so it is very hot.
When ready to serve, sift a thick layer of brown sugar on top.
Put the dishes under the griller until the top is speckled with brown and the cream has melted. Serve immediately while hot. You will find there will be quite a lot of creamy red sauce around the figs.

Chocolate Mascarpone Indulgence

A gorgeous cake which makes no pretence of being anything but totally indulgent, with its rich layers of chocolate mascarpone between light sponge layers. It keeps particularly well — if you can prevent your family from eating it all — improving after 12 hours. It is even better several days later.

Cake	**Filling**	**To finish the cake**
4 eggs	125 g dark chocolate, finely chopped	1/4 cup water
3/4 cup castor sugar	4 egg yolks	1 tablespoon sugar
1 teaspoon vanilla	3 tablespoons castor sugar	2 tablespoons brandy
2 tablespoons cocoa	500 g mascarpone	
1/3 cup cornflour		
1/4 cup plain flour		
1 teaspoon baking powder		

To make the cake
Preheat the oven to moderate (180°C).
Butter the sides and base of two 20 cm cake tins. Line the base with non-stick baking paper.
Separate the eggs and beat the whites in an electric mixer until stiff. Add the sugar and beat for at least 5 minutes or until very thick and the mixture holds a shape when the beaters are lifted. Add the vanilla and egg yolks, one at a time. Sift the cocoa with the cornflour, flour and baking powder and fold through gently. Put into the cake tins and bake in the preheated oven for about 20 minutes or until the cakes are firm to the touch on top and slightly shrinking away from the sides. Leave to cool in the tins for a few minutes and then invert onto a rack to cool. Peel away the paper.

To make the filling
Put the chocolate in a bowl over a saucepan of simmering water, and leave to melt. Allow to cool slightly. Whisk the egg yolks and sugar together and add the mascarpone, stirring until smooth. Lastly, add the chocolate and mix everything together very well. Then chill until firm enough to spread.

To assemble and finish
Heat the water with sugar until it is clear. Boil until syrupy, remove and add the brandy.
Cut each cake into halves, using a sharp serrated knife.
Put one piece of cake onto a plate and brush the top with the syrup, then spread with a little of the mascarpone filling. Put a second piece of cake on top, then spread with more syrup, and more mascarpone. Repeat this procedure with the third layer. Finally, top with more cake, syrup and the rest of the mascarpone, extending it down the sides of the cake.
Decorate with some candied violets, curls or shavings of chocolate or a piping of melted dark chocolate.

Jamaican Bananas

Simmer some orange juice and brown sugar to give a light caramel sauce. Then add thickly sliced bananas, pour in lashings of rum, and you have a spicy, hot dessert with all the romance of a calypso.
Served with ice cream, this is enough for 6.

1 large cinnamon stick
1 piece vanilla bean
½ cup orange juice
¼ cup brown sugar
30 g unsalted butter

6 bananas
¼ cup white rum
¼ cup brown rum

Method

Put the cinnamon stick, vanilla bean, orange juice and brown sugar into a large frying pan. Warm gently, covered, until the sugar has dissolved and add the butter. Cut the bananas into thick slices on the diagonal. Add to the pan and cook for a couple of minutes, turning the banana over so it cooks evenly. It should be a little on the firm side rather than very soft. Pour in both kinds of rum, turn up the heat and cook quickly for a minute. Serve hot, over or around ice cream.

Pears with Red Wine, Basil and Walnuts

Tomatoes with basil, as we all know, is one of the great combinations of the kitchen. And while it may sound odd, pears with red wine, basil and nuts is another complex but extraordinarily good mix of flavours.
This makes 6 serves.

12 large walnut halves
2 cups light red wine, such as a pinot
$^2/_3$ cup sugar
1 piece cinnamon stick, 2.5 cm long
4 strips lemon rind
6 firm pears
12 large leaves of fresh basil

Method
Put the walnuts into a saucepan, cover with water and cook gently for about 5 minutes. Remove and peel as soon as they are cool enough to handle — a tedious job, but, believe me, it makes a difference to the dish.
Put the wine, sugar, cinnamon and lemon rind into a saucepan and warm gently, giving an occasional stir while you are peeling the pears. Cut these into halves lengthwise.
Slide the pears into the saucepan and, if any are protruding from the liquid, spoon some over them, so they won't discolour. Cover and cook over a low heat for about an hour or until quite tender.
Insert a fine skewer into the pears to check that they are soft. When they are, carefully remove them to a bowl, covering with a plate.
Add the basil to the wine and cook until it has reduced by about a third, then pour through a sieve over the pears.
Add the nuts, pushing them underneath the liquid so they will pick up the wine flavour and colour. Leave the pears to mellow in their gloriously red, aromatic sauce for 24 hours before serving.
Cut the pears into thin slices, leaving them attached at top but fanning out slightly to show the variation in colours.
These pears keep beautifully for five days.

Candied Citrus Tart

Glazed and glistening, candied slices of lemon and orange sit on a citrus cream custard in a delectable, tangy tart. It is best to make the candied peel first as it needs to cool completely, and can be stored for several days. Note, too, that it must be soaked in salty water for 12 hours before cooking.

Candied peel	Pastry	Citrus custard
1 lemon	1¼ cups plain flour	3 eggs
1 orange	½ teaspoon baking powder	¾ cup sugar
1 teaspoon salt	pinch salt	¼ cup lemon juice
1 cup sugar	125 g butter	2 tablespoons orange juice
2 cups water	1 egg yolk	grated rind of 1 orange
2 tablespoons Grand Marnier	1 or 2 tablespoons lemon juice	grated rind of 1 lemon
		½ cup cream

To candy the peel
Slice the lemon and orange (with the peel still on) extremely thinly and discard the thick peel at either end of the fruit. Put the slices into a bowl, and cover with cold water. Add a teaspoon of salt and leave to soak for 12 hours.
Drain and gently rinse. Heat the sugar with water in a large frying pan. Add the slices of citrus and cook over the lowest possible heat until the peel on the slices has gradually become translucent and the sugar syrup is thick. If the peel is still tough and the syrup is too heavy just pour in another cup of water and continue cooking. When the peel is tender, add the Grand Marnier. Remove from the heat and leave to sit for 20 minutes. Put the peel on a plate, cover with plastic-wrap and leave aside.

To make the pastry
Blend the flour, baking powder and pinch of salt with the butter in a food-processor. When crumbly, add the egg yolk and lemon juice and process until it forms a ball. Remove and form into a round shape. Flatten this and wrap in some plastic-wrap. Rest for 20 minutes. Roll out between waxed paper and line the base of a 23 cm pie dish. Butter some foil, and press into the pastry, buttered-side-down, along the base and up the sides and bake in a moderate oven (180°C) for 20 minutes, or until set. Remove the foil carefully and return to the oven for 5 minutes to dry the crust. Leave to cool for a few minutes while mixing the custard.

To make the custard and assemble
Beat everything well in a bowl, using a fork or whisk.
Pour the filling into the base. If the base has shrunk and you have too much custard, keep a little aside as you need to allow space for the citrus. Arrange the citrus slices on top of the filling. Bake in a moderate oven 25 minutes or until just barely set to the touch. It will firm more once it has cooled slightly. Remove and either serve tepid or cold, sprinkled with icing sugar if you wish. It keeps for several days.

La Grande Passion

Melting and light, this bavarois uses the sexiest new liqueur on the market, La Grande Passion. Based on fresh passionfruit, its scent and savour linger and seduce the palate. Even better, this is one of the easiest of desserts to make. Serve with a glass of the liqueur alongside, more passionfruit to emphasise the flavours, and some simple little buttery biscuits on the side or some almond bread.
This makes 8 servings.

8 passionfruit
4 tablespoons La Grande Passion liqueur
1 tablespoon gelatine
¼ cup cold water
4 eggs
½ cup castor sugar
1 cup cream, lightly whipped
6 additional passionfruit
a little additional La Grande Passion liqueur

Method
Cut the passionfruit into halves and remove the flesh. Put it into a food-processor and blend for a few seconds. Push through a sieve, so you just have the juices, and mix with the liqueur.
Put the gelatine into a cup with the water, stir and stand this in a saucepan of simmering water. Leave until dissolved and clear.
Separate the eggs and put the yolks into a bowl with the sugar. Beat until thick. Mix in the passionfruit and liqueur and the gelatine, and stir through.
Whip the whites until they hold stiff peaks and mix into the whipped cream. Fold both as evenly as possible through the passionfruit base.
Rinse out a large mould with a capacity of about seven cups or use eight individual moulds that have been lightly rinsed with water.
Chill for at least 4 hours, preferably overnight, to set. To unmould, run under warm water and invert onto a plate or onto individual plates.
Serve with the pulp of the additional passionfruit around the base and a tiny glass of the liqueur for each person.

Apple and Pear Harvest Pie

The bounty of the orchard is reflected in this rustic pie, thick with apples and pears, first baked in a buttery caramel sauce and then enclosed in a light, meltingly tender pastry crust with a crunchy, sugary top. Heavenly served with lashings of plain or whipped cream. Enough for 8 generous servings.

Apple and pear filling
1 kg Granny Smith apples
3 pears
60 g unsalted butter,
  cut into small pieces
$\frac{1}{3}$ cup brown sugar
$\frac{1}{2}$ teaspoon cinnamon
1 tablespoon lemon juice

Pastry crust
$1\frac{1}{2}$ cups flour
$\frac{1}{2}$ teaspoon baking powder
185 g butter, cut into small
  pieces
pinch salt
2 tablespoons castor sugar
2 tablespoons lemon juice

To finish
$\frac{1}{4}$ cup sultanas
$\frac{1}{4}$ cup chopped pecan nuts
2 tablespoons milk
  or cream
sugar

To make the filling
Preheat the oven to moderate (180°C).
Peel, core and thickly slice the apples. Peel, core and cut the pears into quarters. Put the apples into a shallow ovenproof dish, with the pears on top. Scatter with butter pieces, sugar and cinnamon. Then pour the lemon juice over the fruit, and bake in the oven for about 20 minutes or until juices have formed.
Turn the mixture over with a spoon, return to the oven and cook for a further 20–25 minutes, until the fruit is lightly coloured and soft. Leave to cool.

To make the crust
Put the flour, baking powder, butter, salt and sugar into a food-processor and blend until crumbly. Add the lemon juice and process until the mixture can be formed into a ball. Remove and mix, then roll into a ball. Flatten this down and divide into halves.

To assemble and finish
Roll one half of the pastry out thinly between waxed paper and line the base of a 20 cm pie dish with it. Scatter with the sultanas and nuts. Fill with the cooked apple and pear, along with any juices in the dish. Roll out the remaining pastry and place on top, sealing well at the edges and cutting away any excess. Decorate if you wish with pastry 'leaves' (see Note). Brush the top with a little milk or cream and scatter with sugar.
Bake in a moderate oven, (180°C), for about 35 minutes or until a deep golden-brown. Leave the pie to rest for at least 15 minutes before cutting it. It can be reheated. This is best done in a moderate oven, with a piece of foil resting lightly on top of the crust so it won't brown too much.

Note: If you want to add pastry leaves you'll need to make half as much again of the pastry quantity above, and keep aside. Roll this out and cut into leaf shapes, marking veins with a fine knife.

Chocolate Mile High Pie

First made famous in New Orleans, the original Mile High Pie had a crusty base filled with ice cream and an outrageously extravagant pile of meringue on top, so tall it could barely stand upright on the plate.

This version has the same theme but a different combination: a soft champagne pastry, a rich chocolate filling and the lightest, highest meringue possible. It is even better with lots of whipped cream and if you like, a few berries.

Surprisingly, considering it has a meringue topping, I find it holds up well for several days. It cuts into 10 generous portions.

Biscuit base
1½ cups self-raising flour
3 tablespoons cornflour
pinch salt
3 tablespoons castor sugar
90 g butter, cut into small
  pieces
1 teaspoon vanilla essence
1 egg yolk,
3 tablespoons milk

Chocolate orange fudge
  filling
125 g dark chocolate,
  roughly chopped
90 g unsalted butter,
  cut into pieces
¼ cup sugar
¼ cup flour
3 eggs
grated rind of 1 large orange
1 tablespoon Grand Marnier
½ cup cream

Meringue
6 egg whites
pinch salt
½ teaspoon cream of tartar
8 tablespoons castor sugar
2 tablespoons flaked
  almonds

To finish
some icing sugar

To make the base
Butter the base and sides of a 23 cm pie dish.
Preheat the oven to moderate (180°C).
Sift the flour, cornflour and salt into a bowl.
Cream the sugar and butter until fluffy and add to the flour with the egg yolk and vanilla.
Add a little milk and mix with your hands until a soft dough. Either roll out or press into the pie dish.
Prick the base and cover with a sheet of non-stick baking paper. Press it down gently but firmly.
Bake for 20 minutes in the preheated oven, then carefully remove the baking paper and cook for a further 5 minutes or until slightly dried out.
Leave to cool for 15 minutes before placing the filling into the crust.

To make the filling
Put the chocolate and butter into a bowl and stand over a saucepan of simmering water until melted. Stir until smooth.
Beat the sugar and flour with the eggs, orange rind and Grand Marnier until blended but not frothy. Then add the cream and chocolate and mix through.
Pour into the baked tart shell and cook in a moderate oven for 15 minutes or until just barely firm to touch. Be careful not to cook too long as it will firm more when it cools.

To make the meringue and finish the pie

Beat the egg whites with a pinch of salt and cream of tartar until they hold stiff peaks. Very gradually add the sugar, beating until the whites are very stiff and slightly shiny. Spread over the filling, piling it very high in the centre and making sure it is well sealed on the edges. Scatter with almonds.

Return to the oven and bake for about 15–20 minutes or until the meringue is tinged with brown and set to the touch. Remove and cool for about 4 hours before serving, but don't refrigerate or the meringue will sweat.

Just before serving dust lightly with some sifted icing sugar.

Boozy Apple Slices in Apricot Sauce

Generously laced with Grand Marnier and brandy, the apple slices are coated with a rich yet tart sauce made from dried apricots and orange. The only tricky part about making this dessert is to watch the apple slices as they are cooking in the frying pan so they become lightly tinged with colour on the base yet don't caramelise so much that they burn. Best either hot or warm, but this dessert does reheat very well.
Even nicer with a little running cream poured over the top to give a cold contrast.
This makes 4 small servings

---

¹/₂ cup dried apricots
¹/₂ teaspoon grated orange rind
¹/₂ cup orange juice
¹/₂ cup water
2 tablespoons sugar
4 large apples, such as Granny Smith
60 g unsalted butter
¹/₃ cup sugar
piece vanilla pod
¹/₄ cup Grand Marnier
2 tablespoons brandy

Method
Put the dried apricots and orange rind with the juice and water into a saucepan, cover and cook gently for about 10 minutes or until softened. Add the sugar and stir so it dissolves. Purée the mixture, in which there will still be little bits of fruit, and leave aside.
Peel and core the apples, and cut into thick slices. Melt the butter in a large heavy-based frying pan and put the apples into this. They should fit snugly in one layer. Scatter the sugar over the top, and put the vanilla bean into the mixture. Leave them to cook very gently for about 10 minutes, giving the pan an occasional shake and turning them over if they are catching. Then cover the pan with a lid or a large plate.
The apples should form a syrup as they cook, but if you find they are catching on the base add a couple of tablespoons of water. Leave to cook for about 10 minutes or until soft. The cooking time will vary considerably according to the apples.
Pour the apricot purée over the top and gently shake the pan so the apricots sink between the apples. Heat uncovered until bubbling and then tip in the Grand Marnier and brandy. Shake so they coat the top. Remove immediately from the heat and serve.

Note: If there is not sufficient liquid around the dried apricots you can add a little more orange juice after they have cooked.

Mississippi Mudcake

Recipes for this fashionable new chocolate cake are more numerous than the bends in the Mississippi River itself. But as long as the cake has a swampy, sticky, dark appearance and appears to be totally decadent it qualifies. This version is all of those things — and draws chocoholics in like quicksand.
It cuts into about 20 or more pieces.

Cake
1¼ cups strong black coffee
250 g unsalted butter, cut into small pieces
200 g dark chocolate, cut into small pieces
2 cups sugar
½ cup port
¼ cup brandy or bourbon
2 cups plain flour
1 teaspoon bicarbonate soda
pinch salt
2 eggs
½ teaspoon vanilla essence

Topping
2 tablespoons cream
60 g unsalted butter, cut into small pieces
185 g dark chocolate, finely chopped

To make the cake
Preheat the oven to moderate (180°C).
Butter the base and sides of a 23 cm cake tin. Line the base with non-stick baking paper.
Put the coffee, butter and chocolate into a bowl and leave to melt over a saucepan of simmering water. Remove and add the sugar and stir well. Let cool for a few minutes.
Pour into a very large bowl and add the port and brandy or bourbon. A little at a time, sift the flour, bicarbonate soda and salt over the top and beat well with a wooden spoon.
Beat the eggs and the vanilla together for 30 seconds, using a big spoon. Pour into the prepared pan. Smooth the top and bake for 1–1¼ hours. A skewer inserted into the centre should come out slightly moist. Be very careful not to overcook this cake.
Leave it to cool in the pan. It will settle and firm up more. Carefully turn out onto a serving plate.

To make the topping
Put the cream and butter into a saucepan and heat until the butter has melted and bubbles form on the edges. Add the chocolate and immediately remove from the heat.
Shake the pan gently so the chocolate is covered with the hot butter and cream. After a minute stir, cool slightly and then either use to accompany the cake or pour over the top of the cake and spread to the edges to make a rich icing. Allow to set.
This can be accompanied by some berries in season to cut the richness.

Moroccan Orange Salad

Morocco, land of mysterious casbahs and marble palaces, of carved plasterwork with hand-cutting as fine as old lace — a fertile place where oranges, dates and nuts grow in abundance. Try this exotic Moroccan orange salad. The slight tartness of the oranges makes a fresh contrast to the charm of big, plump, fresh dates, aromatic rosewater and pistachio nuts — conjuring up the land of 1001 nights.
This makes sufficient for 4 people.

6 oranges
12 big dessert-style dates
$1/3$ cup orange juice
2 tablespoons lemon juice
2 tablespoons icing sugar
1 teaspoon rosewater
a little cinnamon
some peeled pistachio nuts

Method
Peel the oranges and remove all the white pith. Cut each orange into very thin slices, flicking out any seeds. Cut the dates into about four, removing the seeds.
Arrange the slices of orange in a bowl and then scatter on some date pieces, more orange and more date. You should have a few pieces of date on top.
Mix the orange juice with the lemon juice, icing sugar and rosewater, and pour over the top. Shake the bowl gently so the liquid flows through. The salad may look a little dry at this stage.
Chill, covered, for at least 6 hours but preferably overnight. This will allow lots of juice to form.
Scatter the top with a little cinnamon and then some pistachio nuts. The amount will depend on whether you have a wide or a deep bowl. There should be just a light sprinkle of green.

Winter

A time for puddings, for comforting, warming dishes to finish a meal, nostalgic reminders of childhood, or cool desserts with hearty flavours and satisfying textures.

Fruit Mince Pudding

Made with fruit mince and citrus, this sticky brandied pudding is, perhaps surprisingly, at its best when served cold. However, it has all the rich character of a hot Christmas fruit pudding, but is easier to prepare and lighter to eat. It is served with citrus brandy cream. It makes 10 servings.

Pudding
125 g butter
$^3/_4$ cup castor sugar
6 eggs
grated rind of $^1/_2$ lemon
grated rind of $^1/_2$ orange
$1^1/_2$ cups fruit mincemeat
$1^1/_4$ cups breadcrumbs made from stale
  white bread
60 g ground almonds
4 tablespoons brandy

Citrus brandy cream
grated rind of $^1/_2$ orange
grated rind of $^1/_2$ lemon
2 tablespoons brandy
1 tablespoon lemon juice
$^1/_3$ cup castor sugar
1 cup cream

To make the pudding
Preheat the oven to barely moderate (170°C).
Butter the base and sides of a soufflé dish that holds six cups. Line the base with non-stick baking paper and lightly butter this again.
Cream the butter with the sugar, using an electric mixer, until very light and fluffy. Separate the eggs and add the yolks, one at a time. Mix in the lemon and orange rind and stir. Put the fruit mince into a separate bowl with the breadcrumbs, almonds and brandy, and stir. Add to the egg base and mix everything together. Beat the whites until they hold stiff peaks and fold through, a third at a time.
Put into the prepared dish, cover the top loosely with foil, and bake in the oven for 30 minutes or until just set on top. It will be firmer on the edges than in the centre, which may appear soft. Remove and leave to cool in the container. Then run a knife around the sides and carefully invert on a serving plate.
Serve cut into wedges, accompanied by citrus brandy cream. Or you may prefer to coat the top of the pudding with a layer of the cream.

To make the citrus brandy cream
Mix the orange and lemon rind with brandy, lemon juice and sugar in a bowl and leave to stand for a few minutes to allow the sugar to soften. Whip the cream until it holds stiff peaks and slowly add the citrus brandy mixture, beating with a whisk so it mixes through evenly. It should be fluffy and just barely able to hold a shape. Spread over the fruit mince mould and decorate either with some finely chopped glacé fruit or shreds of blanched lemon and orange rind.

Diplomat Trifle Cake

A creamy dessert, studded with brightly-coloured glacé fruits and laced with Grand Marnier, this is a grand version of a trifle. But unlike that old-fashioned classic, it is set in a basin or a cake tin so it can be cut into wedges. It needs to be refrigerated for 12 hours before serving.

It serves 8 generously and can be as grandly or simply decorated as you wish, depending on the occasion.

The trifle
$^1/_2$ cup mixed diced glacé fruits
$^1/_3$ cup Grand Marnier
1 sponge cake, about 20 cm in diameter
1 cup milk
1 cup cream
4 egg yolks
$^1/_2$ cup castor sugar
grated rind of 1 small orange
1 tablespoon gelatine

To finish
1 cup apricot jam
3 tablespoons brandy
2 tablespoons Grand Marnier

To make the trifle
Put the glacé fruits and Grand Marnier into a bowl and stir. Leave to stand for several hours or overnight.
Line the base of a 20 cm cake tin with some foil.
Cut the sponge cake into smallish cubes, about 4 cm.
Heat the milk and cream in a saucepan until bubbles form on the edges.
Put the yolks and sugar into a bowl and beat until thick. Slowly tip in the hot milk and cream, stirring constantly. Cook until lightly thickened. Don't let it boil. Remove and add the orange rind.
Mix gelatine with about three tablespoons of water. Stir well and add to the hot custard. Stir in so it dissolves. Leave the custard to cool.

To assemble and finish
Warm the jam and add the brandy and Grand Marnier.
Put some cubes of cake into the tin. Dab on some jam mixture. Scatter on some glacé fruits, then pour in about a third of the custard. Add more cake cubes and dab with more jam, more glacé fruits and more custard — until you have used them all. (But keep back a little jam to glaze the top.) Refrigerate for about 12 hours until it has set.
When ready to serve, run a knife carefully around the edge and invert onto a serving plate. Warm any remaining jam and pour through a sieve over the top, brushing out lightly. Be sure the jam is cool before decorating with a little whipped cream and some finely diced pieces of mixed glacé fruit.

Richly Ricotta

A new role for ricotta, with the addition of glacé fruits, lemon juice and ground almonds, it becomes a cake with a light creamy texture and mellow flavours. Don't be tempted to cut it for 24 hours; the longer it is left the better it tastes. It keeps well for about five days if refrigerated. This cuts into 12 portions.

Cake
1 cup sultanas
1/3 cup mixed glacé fruits, finely chopped
4 tablespoons brandy
375 g cream cheese
375 g ricotta
2 tablespoons lemon juice
2 teaspoons grated lemon rind
1/3 cup ground almonds
1/2 cup castor sugar
5 eggs

Topping
3/4 cup sour cream or mascarpone cheese
1/4 cup mixed glacé fruits, finely-diced

To make the cake
Preheat the oven to moderately slow (160°C).
Butter the sides and base of a 20 cm cake tin.
Line the base with non-stick baking paper and butter it.
Put the sultanas and glacé fruits into a bowl, add the brandy and stir. Leave the fruits to marinate for about 20 minutes. Put both kinds of cheese into a food-processor and blend until they are smooth. Add the lemon juice, lemon rind, ground almonds and sugar, and process again. Separate the eggs. Add the yolks, one at a time, to the cheese. Mix through and transfer to a mixing bowl.
Stir in the fruits and any liquid from the bowl in which they were marinated. Beat the egg whites until they hold stiff peaks and gently fold through, a third at a time.
Spoon in the cheese mixture and smooth the top. Bake for about 35 minutes or until firm to the touch on the edges. If it becomes too brown on top rest some foil over the tin.
When cooked the cake should be slightly creamy and soft in the centre. Turn the oven off and leave the cake in the oven for 10 minutes. Remove and let it cool for 30 minutes in the tin. Run a knife carefully around the edge and invert onto a plate. Cover with plastic-wrap and refrigerate for at least 24 hours before cutting, preferably waiting for 48 hours. Let it come back to room temperature before serving so the flavours mellow.
It is best to use a knife that has been warmed in hot water to give a clean slice.

To make the topping
Spread the sour cream or cheese on top of the cake and decorate with the diced fruits. Once it has been decorated it should be eaten within 24 hours.

Spanish Lemon Cake

Fruity and particularly moist, this Spanish cake has no butter. Instead, a fruity olive oil is used, as well as a whole lemon and orange. Cooked first, so they are quite soft, they add an intense tang. A great cake to serve with a bowl of poached fruits or just to enjoy at the end of a meal with a cup of strong coffee.
It cuts into 10 generous pieces.

1 lemon
1 orange
185 g ground almonds
4 eggs
pinch salt
1¼ cups castor sugar
½ cup plain flour
½ cup self-raising flour
1 teaspoon baking powder
½ cup olive oil

Method
Put both the whole lemon and whole orange into a saucepan and completely cover with water. Bring to a boil and drain. Add fresh water, bring back to a boil and cook gently until both are quite tender. Drain and leave to cool.
Cut away both ends of the fruit, then cut the lemon and orange into halves. Scoop out the pulp of the lemon, and discard it. Finely cut up the rind of the lemon and all of the orange, discarding any pips.
Put the fruit into a sieve and shake to get rid of some of the liquid. This pulp could be made hours in advance and stored, refrigerated.
Preheat the oven to moderate (180°C).
Butter a 20 cm spring-form tin. Line the base with some non-stick baking paper and butter it.
Mix the ground almonds into the citrus mixture. Beat the eggs with salt and sugar until very thick and pale.
Sift the flour and baking powder over the top and stir into the eggs. Mix in the fruit pulp and then the oil.
Put the mixture into the tin and bake for an hour until firm to the touch. When cooked, a fine skewer inserted into the centre will come out clean. If the cake is becoming too dark on top, lightly rest a piece of foil over it.
Leave to cool in the tin, and then invert onto a plate and carefully peel away the paper.
You can simply sift some icing sugar over this cake. It really needs nothing else.

New Orleans Apple and Bourbon Pudding

Bread puddings, highly laced and sparked with a heavy mix of egg, milk or cream and bourbon, are a speciality of the jazz centre of the United States. Soft and sweet and high on the list of 'best-ever bread puddings', they have a topping which sets to a sticky glaze. If you don't stock bourbon in your cupboard, brown rum or brandy works just as well. Serves 8.

The pudding
3 Granny Smith apples
$^1/_3$ cup water
2 tablespoons sugar
4 thick slices raisin bread
$2^1/_2$ cups milk
1 teaspoon vanilla essence
3 eggs
$^1/_2$ cup sugar
a little grated nutmeg
1 tablespoon bourbon or brown rum

Bourbon topping
1 egg
2 tablespoons castor sugar
45 g unsalted butter
2 tablespoons bourbon or rum
few drops vanilla essence

To make the pudding
Butter a round or square shallow china ovenproof dish, about 23 cm in size. It should hold five cups.

Peel, core and dice the apples into small cubes. Put them into a saucepan with the water and sugar and cook, stirring occasionally until soft. Put into a sieve and discard the liquid.

Cut the bread into small dice, and place in a basin with the apple. Add the milk and vanilla and leave to stand for about 45 minutes so the bread will soften.

Beat the eggs with the sugar, nutmeg and bourbon. Tip into the apple and bread and stir gently to mix well. Pour into the baking dish and bake in a moderate oven for 25 minutes or until set on top.

Remove and pour the sauce over the top immediately. Leave to rest for about 10 minutes before serving, so the topping sets in a creamy custard.

It can be reheated standing in a baking tin with hot water around, and it also reheats well in a microwave.

To make the topping
Mix the egg and sugar. Melt the butter and add the stir well with a fork. Add bourbon or rum and vanilla.

Chocolate Mince Pudding

Serve it for a June Christmas dinner, or for any special occasion, and its mixture of fruits, chocolate and rum will cut a cosy swathe through the chilliest night. Just to add an even more decadent touch, bring it to the table with a bowl of chocolate brandy hard sauce. It is also delicious with generous scoops of vanilla or brandy ice cream.

This makes enough for 12 because it is the kind of pudding that is best in small serves. You may prefer to make half quantity.

Chocolate pudding
1 cup sultanas
1 cup raisins
1 cup currants
1/3 cup mixed peel
1/3 cup glacé cherries, roughly choppped
1/3 cup chopped dates
1/3 cup chopped prunes
1/4 cup brandy or rum
1/4 cup orange juice
100 g dark chocolate, roughly chopped
1 1/2 cups sugar
6 eggs
1 cup breadcrumbs, made from stale
  bread
1 cup self-raising flour

Chocolate brandy hard sauce
2 tablespoons cream
60 g milk chocolate, cut into small pieces
125 g unsalted butter
grated rind of 1 small orange
3 tablespoons brown sugar
2 tablespoons brandy or rum
generous pinch cinnamon

To make the pudding
Put all the fruits into a bowl. Pour the brandy or rum and orange juice over the top and stir. Cover and leave to marinate for about 24 hours, stirring once or twice.
Butter a pudding basin which holds eight cups.
Put the chocolate into a bowl over a saucepan of simmering water and leave until melted. Beat the eggs and sugar in a large bowl until thick. Stir in the chocolate, fruits and any remaining marinating liquid left in the bowl.
Mix in the breadcrumbs, sift the flour over the top and mix through.
Place into the basin and cover with a double thickness of greaseproof paper, tying it firmly around the edge. Cover with foil and tie this securely. Put into a large saucepan and pour boiling water around it, being careful not to splash any. The water needs to come at least halfway up the sides of the basin. Cover the saucepan.
Cook for 3 hours and check every so often on the water level. If it is dropping too much, add more boiling water.
Remove the saucepan from the heat and leave to rest for 10 minutes. Now take off the lid and carefully remove the pudding.
Run a knife around the edge and invert onto a plate.

To make the sauce

Heat the cream and, when it is bubbling around the edges, add the chocolate. Shake gently and leave a few minutes. Stir. Let it cool to tepid.

Cream the butter with the orange rind and sugar in a food-processor. Next add half the cooled chocolate and cream and then add the remainder. Slowly mix in the brandy, adding the cinnamon last. Remove to a bowl. Fluff the top of the sauce with a fork and serve immediately, or cover and refrigerate. It will become quite hard when cold, so leave out for at least an hour before serving.

Hint: The pudding can be made one week in advance, and reheated. Boil again for 1½ hours when reheating. You can also freeze the butter. It is best to process or whip with an electric beater again before using, so it will be creamy and fluffy.

Melting the chocolate pieces over simmering water.

Beating the eggs and sugar until thick.

Tying up the pudding in a double thickness of greaseproof paper.

Heating the cream and melting the chocolate.

Liqueur Pan Soufflé

Light as a big puffy cloud, this easy pan soufflé relies on a really good liqueur for its flavouring. Use anything ranging from a mandarin or orange liqueur to Galliano or Frangelica, chocolate peppermint or a good cognac. Lovely with some vanilla ice cream or lightly whipped cream but just as good plain. Ideal for 4 people.

30 g hazelnuts
6 egg whites
pinch of salt
4 tablespoons castor sugar
pinch cream of tartar

4 egg yolks
¼ cup liqueur
some icing sugar
15 g unsalted butter

Method

Preheat the oven to hot (200°C). Put the hazelnuts onto a tray and cook for about 6 or 7 minutes, until the skins split. Remove and rub in a tea towel to get away as much of the brown skin as possible. Chop the nuts roughly.

Beat the egg whites with the cream of tartar until very thick. Add half the sugar gradually and beat until glossy. Whisk the egg yolks in a separate small bowl with the remaining sugar and the liqueur. Heat a 22 cm frying pan (with a *metal* handle) and add the butter. Fold half the egg yolks into the whites. Then fold in the remainder, along with the nuts. Pour the soufflé into the pan, leaving some rough peaks on top.

Put the pan on a high flame for about 45 seconds, then transfer to the oven and leave the souflée to cook for about 8–10 minutes, or until puffed and brown. Dust with icing sugar and serve instantly, as it will deflate quickly.

Chocolate Cake with Rum Prunes

A cake which conjures up words like 'decadent', 'divine', 'delicious', it is all of these and more. Prunes, moist with rum and orange juice, give a sticky texture to the cake and toasted hazelnuts, a crunchy one. This cake needs to stand for at least 12 hours, so must be made the day before you want to serve it.
It cuts easily into 14–16 serves and could be halved if you wish.
Serve it plain, with running cream, thick cream or perhaps with ice cream.

½ cup prunes, stoned and cut into small pieces
¼ cup brown rum
2 tablespoons orange juice
400 g dark chocolate, cut into small pieces
250 g unsalted butter, cut into small pieces
6 eggs
1 cup castor sugar
1¼ cups plain flour
pinch salt
100 g hazelnuts, roasted and skinned and finely chopped
icing sugar (optional)

Method
Put the prunes into a bowl, add the rum and orange juice, stir, and leave for 24 hours.
Preheat the oven to moderate (180°C).
Butter the sides and base of a 23 cm cake tin, and line the base with non-stick baking paper. Butter this again. Put the chocolate and butter into a bowl over a saucepan of simmering water and leave until melted.
Put aside to cool slightly.
Separate the eggs and put the yolks into a very large basin. Beat with sugar until pale and thick. Gradually mix in the chocolate and butter, the flour, salt and nuts. Lastly, add the prunes and any remaining liquid.
Beat the egg whites until they hold stiff peaks. Gently fold into the chocolate, a third at a time. Pour into the buttered tin and cook for 25 minutes or until just firm to the touch. It will firm more as it cools.
Remove. Leave to rest for an hour and then run a knife around the edge of the cake tin and gently invert onto a plate. Leave for 12 hours before serving so the cake mellows.
Dust the top with a frosting of sifted icing sugar.

Carrot and Lemon Soufflé Torte

A flourless mixture with a light, melting texture, sweetly laced with carrot and lemon, this has an interesting pink, speckled appearance when it is cut. It needs whipped cream as a foil for the sweetness. This can be left plain or decorated with some tiny shreds of lemon peel or glacéed orange or lemon. It will sink as it cools, but don't be alarmed. This makes the torte settle to a fine texture.
Enough for 10 servings.

250 g carrots
$^1/_3$ cup lemon juice
$1^1/_2$ cups water
$^1/_2$ cup sugar
8 eggs
$^2/_3$ cup castor sugar
grated rind of 1 large lemon
2 tablespoons brandy

Method
Lightly oil a soufflé dish with a capacity of about nine cups. Dust lightly with castor sugar and shake away the excess.
Peel the carrots, grate or shred them and put into a saucepan with the lemon juice, water and sugar. Bring to a boil, cover and cook gently until the carrots have softened. It takes approximately 4 minutes.
Take off the lid and cook the carrots over a high heat until the liquid has boiled away, leaving just a thick syrup around them. Be careful not to allow this syrup to turn to toffee. Let the mixture cool.
Preheat the oven to moderate (180°C).
Separate the eggs, and beat the yolks with the sugar and lemon juice until very thick and pale. Mix in the brandy and carrot mixture, along with any syrup remaining in the pan, and stir through.
Beat the whites until they hold stiff peaks. Fold into the carrot mixture, a third at a time.
Pour gently into the prepared dish and bake in the oven for about 30–40 minutes, or until firm to touch and puffed on top.
Remove and allow to cool for 1 hour, gently pressing down the edges so they are level with the centre which will quickly sink. Run a knife around the edge and invert onto a plate. Cover with some plastic-wrap. The cake can be left like this for up to three days.
Cut into slices, spooning lightly whipped cream on the side of the plate.

Tiramisu

Tiramisu, a traditional Italian dessert, makes no pretence of being anything other than totally indulgent, with its filling of coffee, liqueur, mascarpone custard and grated chocolate. In this version, these ingredients are layered between slices of fluffy sponge to form a voluptuous cake. It makes enough for about 10 thick slices or wedges.

Cake base
3 eggs
½ cup castor sugar
¾ cup self-raising flour
pinch salt
1 tablespoon hot water

Mascarpone filling
4 eggs
½ cup castor sugar
pinch salt
250 g mascarpone

Coffee and liqueur
½ cup very strong coffee,
¼ cup coffee-flavoured
  liqueur or
  an additional
¼ cup strong coffee

Extras
150 g chocolate, finely
  grated
stiffly whipped cream
cocoa

To make the cake
Butter the base and sides of a 20 cm cake tin and line the base with greaseproof paper. Butter this. Preheat the oven to moderate (180°C).
Rinse out your mixing bowl with boiling water, so it is warm. Put into it the eggs and sugar and, using an electric beater, mix for about 10 minutes or until very thick and fluffy. Sift the flour and salt over the top and fold through, along with the hot water. Pour into the prepared tin, shake gently so it spreads out, and bake in the oven for about 18–20 minutes, or until firm to the touch on top and so that it has shrunk slightly from the sides. Leave to rest for 5 minutes in the tin and then invert onto a cake-rack. Let cool completely. If using within the hour, freeze the sponge so it can be cut easily. Otherwise leave overnight to firm.

To make the filling and assemble the cake
Separate the eggs and put the yolks, with the sugar and salt, into an electric mixer and beat well until fluffy and thick. Mix in the mascarpone and beat.
Beat the egg whites separately and fold them into the mascarpone cream.
Cut the cake into four layers. They must be quite thin. Don't worry if any of these break as it won't matter in the finished dessert.
Having washed the tin in which the cake was baked, line the base with baking paper. Place the first layer of cake in the tin. Mix the coffee and liqueur together and generously brush the cake with this. Then add some of the mascarpone filling, followed by a sprinkling of grated chocolate. Repeat this procedure after adding the second and third layers of sponge. Now add the fourth layer, but simply brush it with the coffee and liqueur mixture. Cover and chill for 12 hours before turning out. Top with cream and a dusting of cocoa, then more grated chocolate. Once creamed, it should be eaten the same day. However, the cake will keep for several days, without cream, just covered in the refrigerator.

Lemon Butter Baked Custard

Luscious lemon butter with a buttery country richness is spread onto bread and floats on top of a custard to form one of the great variations of an old-fashioned baked custard, a nostalgic dish which is better than any that Mother ever made.
It makes 8–10 servings.

Lemon butter
90 g unsalted butter, cut into tiny pieces
½ cup sugar
½ cup lemon juice, strained
grated rind of 1 large lemon
2 eggs
2 egg yolks

Baked custard
12 slices white bread
½–⅔ cup lemon butter
3 eggs
2 egg yolks
⅓ cup castor sugar
3 cups milk
1 cup cream

To make the lemon butter
Mix everything together in a basin which will fit over a saucepan. Keep the water underneath constantly simmering. Stir the lemon butter occasionally until the butter has melted and the mixture is tepid. Now stir more frequently until it begins to thicken. Remove and leave to cool. It will thicken more as it becomes cold.
If you are in a hurry, cook directly over the heat, using a whisk and watching carefully. Lift the pan if the base is becoming very hot and the mixture looks as if it may boil. The lemon butter can be stored, covered, for up to four weeks in the refrigerator.

To make the custard
Using a large cutter, about 90 cm in diameter, cut a circle from each slice of bread. Spread thickly with lemon butter.
Put them into a shallow ovenproof dish, about 20 cm in size, so they are slightly overlapping. Beat the eggs with the yolks, sugar, milk and cream and pour through a sieve over the top of the bread. Leave to stand for 10 minutes, then put into a baking tin with boiling water coming halfway up the sides of the dish. Cook for about 45 minutes or until lightly set. Leave to rest for 10 minutes before serving.

Orange and Date Sticky Pudding

The ever-popular sticky pudding has no equal for a chilly winter's evening, with the addition of fresh orange in both the moist pudding mix and in the caramel sauce which is poured over the top. For those who like a generous serve of sauce, the quantities here can easily be doubled. It is almost obligatory to have cream on the side to counteract the sticky sweetness.

This makes 10 serves and reheats very well in a microwave.

Pudding
185 g dates, pitted and cut into small pieces
1 teaspoon bicarbonate soda
¾ cup boiling water
½ teaspoon grated orange rind
¼ cup orange juice
45 g butter
¾ cup castor sugar
2 eggs
1¼ cups self-raising flour

Sauce
¾ cup brown sugar
45 g unsalted butter, cut into small pieces
½ teaspoon orange rind
¼ cup orange juice
¼ cup cream

To make the pudding
Butter a 20 cm square cake tin and line the base with non-stick baking paper.
Put the dates into a bowl with the bicarbonate soda and pour boiling water over the top.
Leave to stand for 10 minutes, then add the orange rind and juice.
Preheat the oven to moderate (180°C).
Cream the butter until soft and then mix in the sugar until light. One at a time, beat in the eggs and then sift the flour over the top. Stir through and add the dates and their liquid. Pour into the cake tin and bake in the preheated oven for about 30–35 minutes or until cooked through. While the pudding is cooking make up the sauce.

To make the sauce
Mix the sugar with the butter and heat until the butter has melted. Add the remaining ingredients and cook over moderate heat for 5 minutes or until lightly thickened. Leave stand a minute. It will thicken a little more.

To serve
Cut the cooked pudding into squares and spoon the sauce over the top.

Acknowledgements

The author and Publishers thank David Jones, Bourke Street,
Melbourne for the generous loan of china and table linen
from their Home Store.
They also thank Barbara and Peter Cuffley for kindly making
their kitchen available for the photograph on pages 90–91.

Index

The Five Mile Press

The Five Mile Press Pty Ltd
22 Summit Road
Noble Park, VIC 3174
Australia

First published 1996
Reprinted 1998

Printed in Hong Kong

National Library of Australia Cataloguing-in-Publication data:

Sutherland Smith, Beverley.
Decadent desserts: spring, summer, autumn and winter.

Includes index.
ISBN 0 86788 568 8
1. Desserts. 2. Cookery (Fruit). I. Title.
641.86